CORRUPTION

JOHNS HOPKINS
UNIVERSITY PRESS

AARHUS UNIVERSITY PRESS

c

o

r r

u

METTE
FRISK JENSEN

t

i o

n

CORRUPTION

Layout and cover: Camilla Jørgensen, Trefold
Cover photograph: Poul Ib Henriksen
Publishing editor: Søren Mogensen Larsen
Translated from the Danish by Heidi Flegal
Printed by Narayana Press, Denmark
Printed in Denmark 2022

ISBN 978-1-4214-4476-5 (pbk)
ISBN 978-1-4214-4477-2 (ebook)

Library of Congress Control Number: 2022930093

Special discounts are available for bulk purchases of this book. For more information, please contact Special Sales at specialsales@jh.edu.

Published in the United States by:

Johns Hopkins University Press
2715 North Charles Street
Baltimore, MD 21218-4363
www.press.jhu.edu

Published with the generous support of the Aarhus University Research Foundation and the Danish Arts Foundation

Purchase in Denmark: ISBN 978-87-7219-183-6

Aarhus University Press
Finlandsgade 29
8200 Aarhus N
Denmark
www.aarhusuniversitypress.dk

PEER REVIEWED

MIX Paper FSC FSC® C010651

CONTENTS

SOMETHING ROTTEN IN THE STATE OF DENMARK

A NIGHTMARE SCENARIO

You are on a hospital ward somewhere in your native country, Denmark. You are with your mother, who has cancer and urgently needs help, but all the doctors and nurses rush by. You beg and plead, but no one gives you a second glance.

Finally you manage to grab hold of a doctor who is willing to clear up the mystery. The staff, refusing to work for the paltry wages they earn in the public health system, will not lift a finger unless somebody pays up front. In other words, you will have to cough up some cash if you want your mother to have any chance of surviving.

You have never heard of this happening in Denmark before. Universal health services have been largely free for all citizens for many years, yet here you are, expected to pay a doctor and two nurses a sum larger than your monthly salary so your mother can receive her vital chemotherapy …

Fast-forward a few hours. You are at a meeting with your son's teacher at his school, and the teacher refuses to hand over his school report. You will have to pay a newly introduced 'release fee' to the head of the school, the teacher explains. And by the way, your son cannot stay enrolled at the school if his report is not picked up and signed for by his parents. You know the fee is illegal, but dare you jeopardise your son's future?

You are in a vaguely Kafkaesque dilemma. Perhaps you ought to report the teacher and the head of the school to the police?

Suddenly your spouse is there, whispering that the police cannot be trusted. The head of the school is the local police commissioner's brother, and everyone knows they support each other when dealing with difficult parents and citizens.

What is more, the police always demand a 'special fee' before they even consider taking action, whether the allegation is assault, rape or kidnapping.

And, your spouse reminds you, even if the case makes it to court, no judge can be trusted to hand down a ruling based on the law of the land. After all, judges are only human, and like the school head and the police commissioner they want to feather their own nests, just a bit. If the right payment is on the table, they can help make incriminating evidence disappear or force witnesses to withdraw unfavourable statements – or make them disappear too.

You now remember reading an outspoken article at the breakfast table that morning. In the daily newspaper *Information* a journalist criticised the public prosecution service for ignoring flagrant breaches of the law, even in the face of irrefutable proof.

The journalist, citing damning evidence in case after case, detailed how the head of the tax authority systematically cut shady deals with top executives from the likes of Maersk, Danfoss and Lego – flagships of the Danish business community – and with former high-ranking politicians from the Social Democrats and the Liberal Party. The journalist also claimed to have proof that an investigation into the defence minister's shareholding in an arms company – from which, representing the Danish Armed Forces, he had ordered four new fighter jets at a cost of almost three billion Danish kroner – had been shelved for no apparent reason.

Your family, friends and colleagues find the article shocking. They have never read anything like it. For as long as anyone can remember, the newspapers and televised media have never been anything but lapdogs to the powers that be. The few brave journalists and public officials who have ever dared to disclose even a crumb of information about the huge personal fortunes of the elite, their seaside mansions north of Copenhagen, or their holiday homes in St-Tropez, have come to a bad end.

At least that is what people suspect, since such critics are never heard of again. All your friends and acquaintances now reckon the same fate will befall the journalist working for *Information*. Writing that article was practically a suicide mission, they say.

Days go by, and each morning you flick through

Information hoping to find news about the affair, or at least some other piece written by the courageous journalist. You find nothing. No news about the case; no by-line with the journalist's name. You eventually pay the special fee for your son's school report. And the Minister of Defence? He is still sitting comfortably behind his nice, big desk …

HERE, THERE AND EVERYWHERE

THE HAPPY COUNTRY

... And suddenly you wake, bathed in sweat. Phew! It was all just a bad dream. Medical treatment is still free, and education and the judicial system are still not for sale to the highest bidder in the welfare state of Denmark, ranked for years as one of the world's least corrupt countries.

However, from a global perspective this remarkable absence of corruption, a noteworthy feature throughout the Nordic region, is an exception. Corruption is commonplace in most countries. What is merely a nightmare scenario for Danes, although frightening enough, is the stark reality in an alarming number of nations around the world.

Whatever its form and scope, corruption is profoundly destructive to any society. If the rule of law does not apply equally to all citizens, and if bribes can pave the way for illegal acts, the result is arbitrary decisions and a lawless society. In a country whose politicians and officials commit malversation, embezzlement and fraud, the general population will lose any desire to follow the rules themselves. The result is a dangerously dysfunctional state. Over recent years social scientists have documented the detrimental effects of corruption, which are, unfortunately, far worse than anyone believed. Corruption dramatically reduces a nation's resources and has dire consequences for value creation and growth, not to mention its adverse affects on general living conditions and health. In many countries these pernicious forces lie at the root of lagging development, daily hardship, water shortages, hunger and poverty.

Much suggests that the level of corruption in a country and its wealth are closely linked. It is hardly a coincidence that Transparency International consistently pegs Denmark high or first on the list of the *least* corrupt countries in the world, while economists rank it is one of the wealthiest. Other research has found Danes to be the world's happiest people. This is probably linked to our trust in one another, as Denmark also has the world's highest level of 'social trust', meaning trust in strangers. In fact, Danes even trust their public administration, including the tax authorities, in their small country, whose 5.8 million citizens also live with one of the world's highest levels of taxation.

AILING STATES

Rogue states, failed states, dictatorships and developing countries are not alone in labouring under corruption. It is everywhere – even in Denmark and similar high-functioning nations.

Consider France, where the former president, Nicolas Sarkozy, has been accused of receiving unlawful political support for his conservative party, the UMP. During the presidential campaign of 2007, Liliane Bettencourt, heiress to the L'Oréal fortune, allegedly passed large brown envelopes filled with millions of euros on to Sarkozy – presumably expecting something in return.

What is more, it is beyond doubt that Sarkozy's predecessor, Jacques Chirac, was tainted. In 2011 he was found guilty of misappropriating public funds while serving as mayor of Paris from 1977 to 1995. In other cases, ordinary police officers, a deputy police commissioner and officials from the prosecution service were found guilty of accepting bribes and abusing their power. Little wonder that 68% of the French population believe corruption is widespread in their country.

Regrettably the situation in France is the rule and Denmark a rare exception. In 2013 an EU-funded research project published a study of corruption levels in its then 28 member states. If all members were like Denmark, together they would have been able to increase their tax revenues by 323 billion euros per year, equivalent to twice the entire EU budget for 2017 – an impressive sum.

But of course, things could be much worse. The vast majority of EU member states rank among the least corrupt third of the world's nations, exceptions being Bulgaria, Romania, Greece and Italy. If anything, this clearly indicates how bad things are elsewhere. In fact, the International Monetary Fund (IMF) has estimated that globally curbing corruption could deliver an additional 1 trillion US dollars in annual tax revenues.

The European Commission has described corruption as a sickness that destroys a country from within. It ruins a people's spirit of enterprise and sense of justice. The will to pay taxes in a country such as Afghanistan, for example, is minimal, since revenues are promptly channelled away to crooked authorities and soon moved to private accounts. Public contracts are often awarded to friends or relatives. The underpaid police officers are on the take, as is the entire judicial system. Politicians are part of the pervasive swindling and deception, and votes can easily be bought or falsified.

CICERO TRIED

Prostitution is often called the world's oldest profession, which may well be true. After all, sex does help make the world go round. Still, in human history corruption probably comes in a close second.

We can read about it in the Bible, first penned a few thousand years ago, so even those who acted as the Lord's earthly scribes must have considered corruption problematic enough to merit prohibition. At any rate, God explicitly warns his prophet, Moses, not to accept bribes, which blind the wise and pervert the words of the righteous (Exodus 23:8). It is deceitful, leading to injustice and 'filthy lucre' – the shameful profits of the personal greed that spawns corruption – so this is no new phenomenon.

The word 'corruption' comes from the Latin noun *corruptio*, meaning 'damage' or 'disease'. In antiquity this word and its Greek counterpart were used to describe moral depravity as seen either in a whole society or in an individual.

Aristotle, Cicero and other thinkers referred to the self-seeking misuse of public funds by civil servants as corruption. In the year 70 BC, Cicero petitioned the courts to punish the Roman politician Gaius Verres, who as governor of Sicily had fleeced the island and its population. During the proceedings the enterprising Gaius Verres tried not only to bribe the jury, but also – unsuccessfully – to install one of his friends as judge, but managed to flee before the verdict was reached. He was therefore found guilty, in absentia, on all counts.

Moral reflections on the topic continued in the sixteenth century with Niccolò Machiavelli. In his 1513 treatise on power, *The Prince*, this Italian diplomat and philosopher described human nature as greedy and power-hungry – in short: corrupt. Human beings were weak and could only be guided back to virtue through strong leadership.

In the late nineteenth century the British historian Lord Acton expressed his view on the dangers of concentrating power: "Power tends to corrupt, and absolute power corrupts absolutely." Corruption was unavoidable since all societies require some form of power-sharing, and Lord Acton saw a correlation between a person's moral ruin and their power: The more power one holds, the slacker one's morals.

Around the same time, the British jurist and historian James Bryce attempted a more precise definition. For Bryce, the bribery of civil servants lay at the very core of corruption, though he also saw nepotism and the abuse of power for personal gain as crucial elements. In so doing he based his analysis on corruption as a political and legal phenomenon, rather than simply a moral issue.

WHERE, WHEN AND HOW?

Over the past 2500 years or so the meaning of 'corruption' has shifted. For the ancient philosophers, societal or personal morality could be corrupted. Bryce's more modern description and narrower definition cover concrete actions by people or states in the way they administrate their responsibilities and exercise their power. This is the definition on which I base my research as a historian.

Twentieth-century scholars and politicians began to divide the phenomenon into two categories – political and administrative corruption – inspired by the German economist and thinker Max Weber's clear-cut distinction between politicians and bureaucrats. Weber held that political corruption takes place in legislative assemblies and parliaments, where the politicians' behaviour or the voting process can be corrupt.

One case in point is Italy's former prime minister, Silvio Berlusconi, who in 2009 and 2013 tabled legislation that would exempt him from prosecution. Other politicians receive millions from corporations to finance their election campaigns. All they have to do is grant public contracts to their benefactors or tweak legislation in their favour.

Weber saw administrative corruption as occurring among civil servants, whose exploits might include embezzling public funds or accepting bribes from a manufacturer to ignore environmental-law violations. They might also take money in return for permits to build on protected land that belongs to, say, a disenfranchised minority – a recurring scenario in the rainforests of Brazil.

Certain types of minor transactions involving government officials and politicians are seen as 'sweeteners' or 'perks' that help 'grease the wheels' of society. Examples are unofficial or extra payments for drinks concessions, passports, driving licences and routine case-handling processes.

But corruption is not the preserve of politicians and public officials. The corporate sector has its own fair share of devious dealings. The building industry is a pet culprit, as I assume most crime-series buffs would agree, but its role in fiction differs little from the real world, where fraud through illegal pricing agreements is just one of many ploys.

Seeking to limit competition and increase profits, some building contractors make clandestine agreements before bidding on a job. This way they can divide and share the market, taking turns at winning contracts by illegally coordinating their bids beforehand.

The world of sports is not pristine either, by any measure. The process of selecting host countries for Olympic Games and world championships seems chronically beset by accusations of corruption, often based on compelling evidence. Many researchers and journalists wonder how Russia could have been chosen to host the

FIFA World Cup in 2018. Allegedly the decision was made after a certain Picasso painting changed hands, with Michel Platini – the former president of the Union of European Football Associations (UEFA) – at the receiving end. Another mystery is how the 2014 Winter Olympics ended up in the Russian coastal resort city of Sochi, ultimately costing seven times more than the 2010 Winter Olympics held in Vancouver, Canada.

Much of the answer is likely found in Transparency International's world list of corruption levels. Canada ranks high on the 2019 index as the world's twelfth-least corrupt country, while Russia comes in 137th, behind Myanmar and other nations with weak track records. Apparently corruption is expensive, since everyone has to have their piece of the pie.

"A BELOVED CHILD ..."

Despite the pervasiveness of corruption, researchers remain unable to agree on a conclusive definition. First consider Denmark, where a chief executive of a local public authority is seen as corrupt if he accepts a weekend holiday from a cleaning company he is about to hire, in his official capacity, for a large contract. Under Danish law, this is a crime that could send him to prison.

Then consider Nigeria or Vietnam, where the lines between bribery, inducement and incentive are far more fluid. The same sort of holiday could be seen as a little treat, just part of the price for a permit to sell cigarettes or build a house. Public salaries are low, and paying a bit extra for a public service is quite common. Many believe this keeps the wheels of their society turning smoothly.

A search for the Danish word *korruption* in the country's penal code yields not a single hit for the word itself. Naturally this does not mean corruption is legal in Denmark. It simply shows that corrupt behaviour is called something else: bribery, embezzlement, fraud, extortion or nepotism, to name but a few. As a well-known Scandinavian saying goes, "a beloved child has many names". If this is true, then – alas! – corruption is a dear child indeed.

Since the 1990s a group of supranational organisations including the World Bank, the OECD, the UN and Transparency International have tried to agree on a definition. "Abuse of entrusted power for private gain" was their joint wording. This is not a bad suggestion, but it is problematic that the word 'abuse' is not clearly defined.

There is little doubt that the authorities in less corrupt countries, such as Sweden or New Zealand, view 'abuse' differently from their counterparts in the world's most corrupt countries, which include Somalia, Afghanistan, Iraq and Sudan. There is simply is no consensus on what 'abuse' is, which takes us back to square one. We evidently have a long way to go before reaching a universal description of exemplary conduct among the world's businessmen, government officials and politicians.

MY GOOD FRIEND SLIM

Since we cannot precisely define or describe corruption, perhaps instead we could try to describe an 'incorrupt' society? This might bring us closer to the sort of 'upright' society that is our goal.

Research has shown that certain traits typify an upright society: due process of law; strong, competent public institutions that are impartial and accountable; and a professional body of civil servants, recruited based not on friendship or kinship but on formal qualifications. In other words, my colleagues and I have identified the very elements that bring better quality to public institutions *and* are key components in what we often call 'good governance'.

If public officials are impartial and treat all citizens equally, no groups or individuals will enjoy special favour. An example of a country where this is not the case is Mexico. In the 1990s one of the world's richest men, Carlos Slim Helú, was a close friend of Mexico's president, Carlos Salinas de Gortaris. As everyone knows, real friends help each other. One of the president's initiatives was especially advantageous for his good friend Slim, namely the privatisation in 1985–2000 of some 1200 state-run enterprises.

When Telmex, the national Mexican telephone monopoly, was privatised, Slim won the tender after a very 'special' process, giving the president's best friend exclusive rights to operate Mexico's telephony for five years. Prices rose more than 200%. Meanwhile, Slim was one of the largest private contributors to the 1994 election campaign for the president and his ruling party, PRI. These arrangements hinted at special treatment and conniving – corruption – at the highest level.

The word 'corruption' is found in virtually all languages, and we can all come up with a euphemism or two for this deceitful phenomenon. Besides 'sweetener' and 'enticement', popular terms include 'compensation', 'gratuity', 'incentive' and 'fee'. Less positive terms are 'money under the table', 'hush money', 'kickback', 'protection money' and a host of others.

Surprisingly, here research lags behind the general population. Although academia still lacks a clear definition, anthropologists have found that most people, across cultures, can quickly identify corrupt behaviour.

Villagers in India regard bribery and self-enrichment by public figures as a negative thing for the same reasons that Danes, the IMF and Transparency International do. These findings allow us to conclude that corruption does not occur because certain cultures or peoples accept it.

Research also confirms that even in very corrupt societies, such as Nigeria, people try to distance themselves from corruption, although usually they have little choice in such matters. To survive, they must use the same dubious methods as everyone else.

A mother in Nigeria, or in Zimbabwe, Yemen or any other country plagued by corruption, who does not pay the doctor a little extra will not get her child vaccinated. A person in Kenya, Venezuela or Uzbekistan who applies for a passport will not with certainty receive it unless their application includes an envelope with an 'extra fee'. A car driver in Moscow who gets pulled over and does not hand the traffic officer a couple of roubles risks being accused of a much graver violation than the one he may, or may not, have committed. Everyone's hands are dirty.

In a society steeped in corruption, it makes no sense *not* to do as everyone else does. Being the only honest police officer, doctor, government official or politician is a hopeless cause. If everyone else is on the take, obviously only one person will miss out because of your honesty: you. The crux of the problem in high-corruption countries like Russia and Bangladesh lies with the political and administrative elite, which is the most corrupt layer of all.

TOP DOGS IN A RACE TO THE BOTTOM

The list of corrupt heads of state and government is impressive. One champion of ill repute is the former Indonesian general and politician Suharto. As president of Indonesia, from 1967 to 1998, Suharto relieved his country of a staggering 30 billion dollars or so. He owned luxury homes in Bermuda, the Cayman Islands and Hawaii, a mansion outside Los Angeles and a ski ranch in New Zealand – an amazing real-estate portfolio on a president's salary.

The former presidents Ferdinand Marcos of the Philippines, Slobodan Milosevic of Serbia and Robert Mugabe of Zimbabwe also rank high on the list of corrupt top dogs. As a telling detail, Imelda Marcos, the former Philippine first lady, was forced to abandon over 1200 pairs of shoes when the population finally got so fed up they drove the presidential couple out of the country in 1986.

Worldwide, roughly 80% of people are adversely affected by, or personally suffer under, hopelessly corrupt institutions. We have already noted how hugely destructive corruption is, and yet we still do not know how to fight it effectively.

Most joint international anti-corruption initiatives over the past 15–20 years have shown discouraging results. Tanzania and Mexico, among others, offer examples of foreign-aid and infrastructure funds being misused, despite donors demanding strict control and accountability. On paper the builders, contractors and associates are keen to itemise all expenses so they tally up.

But amounts used for bribes and kickbacks can be entered in the ledgers as 'building materials', which in turn calls for fake invoices that involve others in the scam. Sometimes local contractors who have won a tender can outsource the work to subcontractors – after taking a cut for acting as 'intermediaries'. In many cases only a fraction of the original funds are spent on actual roads or bridges, which are often so shoddily built that they soon fall apart.

Up and down go the painted ponies on the merry-go-rounds of corruption, which show few signs of stopping any time soon.

Perhaps we still do not fully understand all the many faces and facets of corruption, and so remain unable to stamp it out? Perhaps there is a lack of will, meaning we cannot find a way? Then again, the problem may just be so overwhelming that there is no straightforward solution. When an entire society is infused with corrupt practices, who can take the first step towards change? In the Nordic countries we would probably say: our political leaders, of course. However, in large parts of the world it is not that simple, since, as we have seen, this is precisely where we find the worst culprits – at the top.

GETTING TO DENMARK

Those familiar with Greek mythology will know the legend of Sisyphus, a king who, punished by the gods for sacrilege, was doomed to roll a boulder up a hill forever. Each time his struggles brought the boulder close to the top, it would roll back down. This may be a fitting metaphor for the worldwide battle against corruption.

So what to do? Should we give up trying?

Corruption researchers have lately been studying Denmark to find our how it can have, and maintain, such a low, almost exemplary level of corruption. The aim is to find mechanisms that can help weak states become well-functioning societies. The crucial question being asked by the American political scientist Francis Fukuyama and many others is: How might countries like Nigeria, Yemen and China become more like Denmark?

Instead of just trying to identify what countries rife with corruption have done wrong, scholars are focusing on how to limit corruption. The goal is "getting to Denmark",

Fukuyama's phrase for forging a robust, orderly, smoothly run nation.

Apparently, Denmark did something right along the way. Something special that has enabled us to curb corruption, to some degree. Naturally, the Danes still have corruption and probably always will. The remarkable thing is that we have much less than most other countries. The question is: Why?

The short answer, presumably, is that the top dogs and high fliers – the upper echelons of society – do not generally sink so low as to become corrupt. As a matter of fact, there has been a will in Denmark, and a way, to combat such problems for centuries, going at least as far back as 1660, the year the first king with absolute power sat on the Danish throne.

"Power tends to corrupt, and absolute power corrupts absolutely." If we reconsider Lord Acton's dictum in this light, we must admit there is at least one exception, as Denmark was officially ruled by absolute monarchs for nigh on two hundred years, from 1660 to 1849.

BECOMING DENMARK

A ROYAL AFFAIR

In 1660 the Danish king, Frederik III, successfully introduced the most supreme form of absolute rule Europe had ever seen. The backdrop for this change was quite gloomy, as Denmark had recently lost her Scanian provinces east of the Øresund strait – Skåne, Halland and Blekinge – to her then arch-rival, Sweden, and was on the verge of state bankruptcy. The aristocracy reluctantly had to cede to Frederik III all of the powers that had previously been shared by a council of noblemen and an elected king.

Absolute rule transformed Denmark into a hereditary monarchy. Now the king alone held all power and authority to rule. All decisions on wars, taxation, legislation and other important matters had to be approved by the monarch. Obviously, in practice no king could personally rule his country in every detail. He also needed time to go hunting and meandering, courting and philandering, and so he would delegate certain authorities to his 'civil servants', as the king's officials were called in the late seventeenth century. They would then administrate by proxy, on the king's behalf.

From 1660 onwards Denmark's corps of civil servants became an increasingly well-defined and professional hierarchy under the king. Many of the highest administrative positions in the realm, previously monopolised by the nobility, were eliminated. Instead the king put emphasis on his civil servants' loyalty, competence and skills in writing and arithmetic.

In the latter half of the seventeenth century, Frederik III and his son, Christian V, carefully steered clear of renewed dependency on the nobility. One prerequisite for this independence was a body of civil servants who would not threaten the monarch's absolute power. To this end the kings deliberately recruited the sons of the bourgeoisie, rather than young noblemen. Having no inherited power, influence or family fortunes, this new breed of administrators would depend on their income from serving the crown.

The king needed his loyal civil servants not only to consolidate his new autocratic power base but also to collect taxes. Sweden still loomed large as a military threat, and both Christian V and in particular his son, Frederik IV, aspired to reclaim the lost provinces of Scania.

By the early eighteenth century Denmark and Sweden were probably the two most thoroughly militarised nations in Europe, considering their numbers of troops in proportion to their populations. This called for efficient administration, heavy taxes and a larger, more professional state apparatus. Digging into the national income figures, we can see that tax payments rose dramatically from the mid-1600s and at least through the next century. The main contributors were the tenant farmers, who were bound in villeinage to their land.

IT'S GOOD TO BE THE KING

Civil servants answered directly to the king, and he was responsible for their actions. Each new civil servant would formally pledge allegiance to the Danish king and crown, taking an 'oath of office' that was meant to establish an unbreakable bond between the civil servant and his absolute monarch – who was, after all, believed to sit on the throne by the grace of God.

From 1671, Christian V increased the social status of civil servants by a law of 'governing rank and precedence', which enabled kings to recognise civil servants for loyal service. Suddenly, dutiful subjects in positions of trust could be seen flaunting prestigious titles such as 'royal councillor' and 'state advisor', formerly reserved for wealthy noblemen.

This conclusively confirmed that civil servants could attain the highest positions in the realm's official hierarchy, not least because the king alone appraised his civil servants and could bestow rank and title, at his discretion, on low-born and high-born alike. Both principles doubtless strengthened the social standing of civil servants in Denmark, making such positions even more attractive.

The benefits of this arrangement were mutual. The Danish king got a corps of fairly loyal deputies, and the civil servants gained a status they could only have dreamt of prior to 1671. The king had the top hand, though, for if, at any time, for any reason, he was not satisfied, he could remove any civil servant from his position. Rank, title, power and influence were merely on loan.

One can only speculate as to how the constant risk of dismissal affected the civil servants' work, but likely they would have been keen to fulfil the king's wishes while making few independent decisions.

Nowadays we Danes celebrate innovation and entrepreneurial spirit. In the age of absolute monarchy in Denmark, peasants passing the town gates to sell their potatoes, turnips and cabbages at the market would hardly have appreciated customs officers with a talent for inventing new tasks for themselves or new taxes on farm produce. And as for the customs officers, their job was simply to enforce the king's laws.

GRIFFENFELD'S GRAFT

In the year 1676, Frederik III's private secretary, Peter Schumacher Griffenfeld, who had been promoted to 'chancellor of the realm', was removed from office and placed under arrest. Eleven years earlier he had helped draft the Danish constitution of 1665, the 'King's Law', which consolidated the absolute monarchy. Now here he was standing trial before a special 'commission tribunal', charged with nepotism, systematically selling ecclesiastical and secular offices, taking bribes and other misconduct.

Using his position as chancellor – second in power only to the king – he had also installed numerous family members in key positions. His sister's husband was lord mayor of Copenhagen; another brother-in-law worked at the royal commerce office; his cousin was secretary of the Danish chancellery, the equivalent of the department of state and justice; and his younger brother was postmaster general.

Griffenfeld was also found guilty of accepting what he described – while arguing his case before the commission tribunal – as "gifts of gratitude". Today we would call this bribery.

Before Griffenfeld's trial, Denmark had no law against civil servants accepting bribes. This was remedied with a royal decree dated 20 March 1676 that prohibited "the giving and receiving of coin and gift" and introduced the death penalty for such transgressions. This was the first legal measure denouncing a practice that had probably been relatively common. A few years later Griffenfeld's sentence was commuted to life imprisonment.

During the eighteenth century the ban on bribery was often reiterated and reinforced, clearly signalling that corruption à la Griffenfeld would not be tolerated, even if the offender happened to be one of the king's closest retainers.

A SOLEMN VOW

Until the mid-1700s civil service was mainly a practical line of work. Aspirants were educated 'by the pen', often working as scribes or transcribers for civil servants and learning about administrative practices and Danish law before seeking an office from the king.

As tradition dictated, many seventeenth-century civil servants from the aristocracy would have attended either the Royal Academy for Young Noblemen in Copenhagen or Sorø Academy, west of the capital. They would then have followed in their fathers' and grandfathers' footsteps, completing their studies abroad at European universities such as Göttingen, Leipzig, Paris and Oxford.

In 1736 it became possible to study jurisprudence – law – at the University of Copenhagen, after which Danes who lacked the money or opportunity to study abroad could earn a law degree in Denmark and pursue a career as a civil servant. Over time, more and more administrative positions went to graduates from the University of Copenhagen. Uniformity of education was a key factor in professionalising the civil service. It helped to develop a Danish state apparatus that relied on the rule of law, since those who worked there were well versed in the laws of the land. In the parlance of their day, the king's civil servants became 'learnèd in law'.

Actually, it was not until the early 1800s that most civil servants held formal qualifications in law. After this time and until the early 1900s, men with law degrees had a virtual monopoly on high-level positions in the state administration. They have since been joined by colleagues, no longer exclusively male, with more varied backgrounds in political science, economics, and even history and similar 'soft' fields.

For the Danish monarchs of the 1700s and 1800s the ideal civil servant was a university-educated jurist. Such an administrative corps, with its expansive knowledge of law, could apply legal principles to more and more areas. What is more, their excellent schooling meant the king could set even more exacting standards.

Their tasks came to be described in ever-greater detail in instructions and other documents given to new appointees. Over the years this made Denmark's administrative practices more consistent, and – an equally important point – minimised the scope for corrupt personal conduct. Although by no means comparable to today's high standards for public administration, in its day this promoted the emergence of a bureaucratic framework based on law and justice.

In fact, a line can be drawn from 1736 to the present day. Since that year, every law graduate in Denmark has taken an oath, implicitly or explicitly, to abide by certain ethical principles in their work, notably "never to stray from justice and impartiality".

THE SHRUNKEN TREASURY

The legal practices of the 1600s and 1700s fundamentally influence the low level of corruption in Denmark today, and research unanimously points to clear links between corruption and the way a national administration recruits its public officials.

Crucially, government officials must be employed based solely on their professional qualifications. As soon as family background or political persuasion starts to play a part, researchers like myself detect a rise in corruption, as such officials tend to be more concerned with catering to special interests than making sound decisions for the whole nation.

That is why, even from a modern perspective, it was incredibly clever of Denmark's kings to insist that civil servants were only acting by proxy on the monarch's behalf. They could be removed at any time if they failed to act in the king's best interest. Somewhat predictably the absolute monarchs themselves were unable to resist the temptation to occasionally resort to more or less problematic methods, including the sale of public positions.

In this respect Frederik IV was no saint, making the most of his right to appoint civil servants to supplement Denmark's shrunken treasury. In 1700–1701 alone he sold no fewer than 47 positions with such titles as district revenue officer, bailiff and customs officer. He also sold several administrative posts in districts in Norway, which was part of the Dano–Norwegian realm until 1814.

We have also found documents confirming that, once again, things were rotten in the state of Denmark around 1715–1716, when Frederik IV sold a total of 56 positions for offices including district and city bailiff, district and city scribe, mayor and alderman. Most of the revenue from the first round helped foot the bill for Denmark's involvement in the Great Northern War (1700–1721) between Sweden and a coalition of Russia, Denmark and Poland. The proceeds from the second round were spent on a new building for the central administration, completed in 1721 and located next to the king's castle in Copenhagen. It now holds the offices of the Ministry of Finance – a poetic end for an edifice built with funds from a manoeuvre which, today, would be called corrupt.

THE DISINFAMOUS AND CREDITABLE

Denmark's kings demanded much of their civil servants. According to the Danish Law of 1683, a national legislative milestone adopted under Christian V, judges had to be both *uberygtede* and *vederhæftige* – 'disinfamous' and 'creditable'.

'Disinfamous' meant that to be in the king's civil service, one must never have been found guilty of, or admitted to, any action the public would consider reprehensible. Being 'creditable' meant that one had not incurred an insurmountable debt.

This was a wise move by Christian V and the civil servants who drafted the law. The temptation to pilfer crumbs from the kingdom's pie would doubtless be smaller for people who had a firm grip on their personal finances. Furthermore, civil servants in towns and rural areas had to have enough money to make payments in advance, on behalf of the public authorities, since Denmark still had no organised network of reliable financial institutions.

Another royal demand was that all tax collectors in the country must account for income and expenses to the 'royal exchequer' in Copenhagen. On top of that, new customs officers and civil servants in the local districts had to provide 'surety' when taking up their position, posting a guarantee equivalent to a full year's income.

The ruling class believed these legal provisions would ensure accountability and correct entry of income and expenses in the ledgers, knowing that local officials ran the risk of personally having to cover any shortfalls. The measures also gave the officers managing the national budget in Copenhagen a more effective hold on civil servants around the country.

THE SHADOWLANDS OF CORRUPTION

Despite all efforts, bad apples kept appearing in the king's corps of civil servants.

In 1725, Frederik Rostgaard, head secretary in the Danish chancellery, was summoned to appear before the court, accused of accepting 'coin and gift'. Rostgaard, a man of high standing, had held a series of prominent positions, having once served as a judge on the supreme court and as the director of the Danish West India–Guinea Company. Frederik IV had even married Rostgaard's wife's half-sister in 1721, so the two men were effectively brothers-in-law. That may explain, in part, why Rostgaard thought he was above the law of the land.

At any rate, Rostgaard must have realised he was in deep trouble. Shortly before his arrest he sent a petition to Frederik IV admitting that he had accepted "discretion" for various services rendered, but maintaining that he had never "done anything against His Majesty's interests re the acceptance of coin and gift."

Frederik IV showed no clemency. Rostgaard was stripped of all titles and positions and banished from the capital. Ordered to repay all monies he had received, he returned in shame to his manor house, Krogerup, in northern Zealand. Years later, though, he got permission to attend court again and was even appointed chief administrative officer of a region.

Rostgaard is just one example of corruption under absolute rule. Danish researchers have yet to systematically investigate the 1600s and 1700s, so exploring the shadow-lands of corruption among the civil servants of that era may reveal much that is new.

Although Danish corruption researchers may, some day, map out this whole dark, unknown territory, we would still not know for sure whether we had got the full picture. The difficulty is that our options are confined to following the tracks of the civil servants who were discovered and prosecuted, while we have no way of knowing just how many corrupt civil servants went smiling, unpunished, to their graves. Unfortunately we assume, as a rule, that any society has far more corruption than what comes to light. In this respect, contemporary Denmark is no exception.

DEAR KING ...

The absolute monarchs and their laws were not alone in shaping the behaviour of Denmark's civil servants. Religion, we know, also played an important role. One example is found in a little catechism written by the prominent Danish theologian Erik Pontoppidan and published in 1737. Anyone seeking confirmation into the Lutheran faith in Denmark, meaning virtually everyone, had to learn this text by heart to follow tradition and pass into adulthood.

Successive generations of children aged 12–13 became versed in the sinfulness of deceit and fraud. For decades, Pontoppidan's catechism was probably the most widely read book in Denmark. The title itself, *The Truth of Piety*, certainly invites reflection on righteousness, and according to its author the book contains explanations for everything "one who wishes to become blessed" needs to know, and needs to do.

The 1700s saw a surge in literacy among the Danes, who used their new-found skills to write to the king directly. This general 'right to petition', also for common citizens, was part of the Danish Law of 1683. Some letters contain complaints from farmers about local civil servants or administrators. A petition could work almost the same way as a whistle-blower provision does, giving the king and his advisers a better idea of how their local representatives were carrying out their duties.

It is hard to determine the actual effectiveness of two centuries' worth of petitioning against corrupt civil servants. Still, this practice may well have encouraged at least some civil servants to stay on the straight and narrow. After all, they would have to consider the prospect of some pedantic commoner writing a complaint to the king about a mere peccadillo they had committed, potentially forcing them to exchange their easy, agreeable life with a dank, vermin-infested prison cell.

AN EPIDEMIC OF EMBEZZLEMENT

Much was done to counter corruption in the early

nineteenth century, which still saw many and varied examples of power and trust being abused, and civil servants on all levels of Denmark's administrative hierarchy being caught and sentenced.

One problem for civil servants caught with their hands in the cookie jar was that they had become accustomed to dipping – just for crumbs, of course – into the public coffers they were entrusted with safeguarding. Things became so bad, especially in 1810–1830, that the Danes spoke of an actual 'epidemic of embezzlement'.

To some extent this epidemic was attributable to external factors after Denmark became embroiled in the Napoleonic Wars in the early 1800s. When Russia and France joined forces, they made neutral countries like Denmark choose sides. So it was that Denmark became allied with France and Emperor Napoleon, against England.

Due to this ill-fated decision Copenhagen was bombarded by the English fleet, not just once but twice, first in 1801 and again in 1807. Adding insult to injury, Frederik VI was forced to cede Norway to Sweden as part of the terms of peace in 1814.

The war and its aftermath put Denmark in dire economic straits. Inflation was sky-high, and the Danish state actually went bankrupt in January 1813. The royal mint had printed excessive amounts of bank notes during the war, and economic reforms had failed to deliver results. The country's economy was in crisis, and agriculture – Denmark's key production sector – was in sharp decline, which continued into the late 1820s.

These circumstances likely tempted many civil servants beyond their means. Time and again their ordinary salaries were eroded by galloping inflation. An obvious solution was to maintain a respectable standard of living with small loans from the state funds – which might well go unnoticed and unpunished.

A MEMORABLE GETAWAY

Symptoms of the embezzlement epidemic were everywhere. In 1820 one of Denmark's most prominent civil servants stood trial. His name was Christopher Schöller Bülow, and he was the chief administrative officer for the county of Copenhagen and the diocese of Zealand. He was charged with a shortfall of 23,000 *rigsbankdaler*, the national currency at the time, an amount equivalent to several years' salary.

Rather spectacularly, however, Bülow did not end up in prison. He fled in early 1820, before his sentencing, by walking across the frozen waters of the Great Belt between Zealand and Funen disguised as a huntsman and accompanied by his son and a loyal servant. From there he travelled to the still-Danish region of Holstein, where he owned a property, and then to Hamburg, Germany – just beyond the reach of Danish jurisdiction.

This high-profile case was investigated as discreetly as possible by a commission tribunal, but it still caused a stir in Copenhagen. It was not every day such a high-ranking official was caught with his fingers in the till. The affair must also have upset Frederik VI, supreme ruler of the realm and thus responsible for all that went on there, and the first in line for criticism of his system and his civil servants.

The city's gossipmongers and satirical journals had a field day. The affair gave rise to several articles that publicly criticised the moral decrepitude of civil servants and administrators. Prominent publishers and writers called for more vigilance and closer scrutiny, asking that civil servants' accounts be made public, and that citizens be given easier access to complain about decisions. These are some of the very measures corruption researchers are preaching today.

A TIMELY DEATH

The autumn of 1820 brought another notable corruption case in which the chief administrative officer in the county of Ribe, Hans Koefoed, was short some 37,000 *rigsbankdaler*, a stunning amount almost twenty times his yearly salary. The first consequence after the discovery of Koefoed's shortfall was that he lost his position pending an investigation, once again conducted by a commission tribunal.

Koefoed explained to the tribunal that he had been a wealthy man when he took up his post in 1811. Regrettably the economic crisis, inflation, and the dramatic drop in land and property prices had depleted his personal funds so severely he had been obliged to borrow from the local treasury.

In a modern context this sounds like an open-and-shut

case again Koefoed. Today, Danes are brought up to believe in watertight doors between any official's public role and personal finances, but that was not the case in 1811. Civil servants like Koefoed could borrow entrusted funds to tide them over, as long as they could repay them when notified of an official audit – which only happened at irregular intervals.

This practice was hard to manage, particularly during Denmark's economic crisis. While under investigation Koefoed repeatedly wrote to the king to explain his situation, but to no avail. He was found guilty as charged, lost his position and was ordered to repay the deficit. This was beyond his means, so he was set to appear before the supreme court – but ended up dying before the trial.

THE EPIC SCAM OF CHRISTIAN BIRCH

One of the biggest fraud cases in the history of Danish public administration also occurred during this period. It revolved around a powerful, well-connected civil servant named Christian Birch, who was just steps away from becoming the country's finance minister.

From his position as secretary at the ministry of finance, Birch was responsible for issuing Denmark's government bonds. In 1802 he secretly set aside a batch of bonds for himself, then pledged them, but continued to collect the interest. His profits were astronomical: over a million *rigsbankdaler*, some 660 times his annual salary.

So where did all this money go? We can only speculate, but if Birch had spent it to keep up a lavish lifestyle, his scam would probably have come to light sooner. Apparently he was a gambling addict and lost it all on playing the state lottery. At his trial years later, Birch argued in his defence that the 'borrowed' public funds had gone directly back to the treasury, so the judges ought not consider his actions to be punishable offences. The court and king did not share this view.

Birch explained that his financial woes began when Christiansborg Castle, then the royal residence, burned down on 26 February 1794. At the time he was engaged to Frederikke Louise Rottbøll, whom he was to wed that spring. Miss Rottbøll, who worked as a reading companion for Juliane Marie, the dowager queen, lived in a room at the castle. The young couple had purchased many items for their future home and stored them in the castle attics.

When the castle was gutted by fire they lost all their valuable furniture, linens, tableware, kitchenware ... everything. To see the wedding through, Birch had to take out a loan of a thousand *rigsdaler*.

That very year Birch had been tasked with overseeing the lottery, which the state had taken over from the Copenhagen lottery company in 1774, passing the proceeds to the national poorhouses and the national treasury.

Birch's new remit taught him a lot about how the numbers lottery worked, and about how probabilities could be calculated, enabling him to bet on numbers that had not been drawn for some time.

The unlucky Birch, finding it hard to pay the instalments on his wedding loan, began to gamble on the numbers, hoping for a 'big win' that would wipe out his debt in one go. By December 1802 he had run out of cash and could no longer stick to his grand plan. That was the first time he 'borrowed' government bonds. Over the next 18 years, his 'loans' escalated until his exploits were finally exposed, in 1820.

The scam and the scandal were of epic proportions, destroying Birch's reputation and casting long shadows on the king, Frederik VI, given that Birch was one of the crown's most trusted civil servants. To make matters worse, Birch's brother was the bishop of Aarhus, his father-in-law the former bishop of Viborg, and his brother-in-law a supreme-court lawyer.

The accused and his wife both begged the king for leniency. In a petition to Frederik VI, now kept in the Danish National Archives, Frederikke Louise Birch appealed to His Majesty's "humanity-loving heart" and hoped the monarch himself would sit in judgment of the case – as an autocratic king could do – instead of having it heard by a normal court of law. Mrs Birch hoped the king would take his 38 years of civil service into account and be magnanimous enough to pass judgment on her husband without involving the regular judicial system.

Birch's own application for a pardon, addressed to the king and likewise found in the Danish National Archives, also stresses how the decades he had spent serving the crown had been "the most troublesome and cumbersome ever to exist for Denmark's public finances." Therefore –

Birch argued – his long service was equivalent to at least 50 years of ordinary civil service.

Birch had been one of just a handful of civil servants who had drafted the finance reform, which was meant to help Denmark recover from the national bankruptcy of 1813. One element of the reform, passed as a decree and implemented without delay, was to replace the existing monetary system of *rigsdaler* with *rigsbankdaler* as the valid currency of the realm. But Birch's impressive credentials did not help him, and a commission tribunal judged him harshly. Embezzlement and fraud in the top of Denmark's public administration could not be tolerated.

THANK THE OLD KINGS

Denmark was still an absolute monarchy in the early 1800s, but the throne of her ruler, King Frederik VI, was no longer so secure.

The country was a shambles. Not only was Denmark bankrupt and labouring under an agricultural crisis; as described earlier, it had also lost massive territories and resources when forced, in 1814, to cede Norway to arch-rival Sweden after supporting France in the Napoleonic Wars. Times were tough for the king and his subjects.

After the French Revolution in 1789, and with it the beheading of Louis XVI, some Danes felt the time of reckoning had come. There *must* be some alternative to an absolute monarch. Revolutionary sentiments were certainly afoot in Denmark, but today the country is proud of its peaceful, orderly transition in 1849 from absolutism to budding democracy. This nice story is something of a myth, however, since at the same time a bloody civil war was going on in the Schleswig-Holstein border region, putting severe pressure on the ruling establishment in Copenhagen.

As mentioned, the king was directly responsible for his civil servants, so denouncing his administration as corrupt was an indirect criticism of the king. Since he held the throne by the grace of God, theoretically the king was infallible, and by extension so were his civil servants. No wonder the monarch and his advisers had to act promptly to ensure his position and the legitimacy of his rule.

Frederik VI's manoeuvring was largely successful, and he remained on the throne until his death in 1839. Absolutism did not formally end until 5 June 1849, when Frederik VII signed the Constitutional Act of Denmark and transformed the country into a constitutional monarchy. Long before this, however, in the late eighteenth century, kings and advisers were already paying at least a modicum of heed to the population's wishes. One example was the agricultural reforms that improved the conditions of near-slavery known as villeinage for tenant farmers who 'belonged' to a landowner. That is why historians often refer to this period as a kind of enlightened autocracy guided by public opinion.

Because of such measures, the corrupt civil servants did not undermine people's fundamental trust in the king and state. Culprits were held accountable, and more and more control measures were introduced.

From 1840 civil servants could no longer borrow from public funds, and a new penal code regulated the administration of state property and the treatment of citizens. Last but not least, civil servants' salaries and pensions were improved, probably making many officials less likely to dip into the till.

Generally speaking, corruption gradually became less frequent from the late 1820s to 1860. Since the mid-nineteenth century it has remained low and fairly stable, with a handful of cases each year.

In other words, corruption in Denmark's public administration was curtailed all of 150 years ago. How ironic, that the equality-loving Danes of the twenty-first century have a line of old, autocratic kings to thank for their modern society, where connections and family ties do not outweigh merit.

For historians studying corruption cases between 1810 and 1830, one particular change clearly comes to the fore. When civil servants of this period were punished, it was for shortfalls and lacking funds, not for bribery, as often seen in the 1700s with Rostgaard and his ilk.

History is no exact science, so historians can only offer more or less plausible explanations of this clear shift. However, much suggests that the absolute rulers' stricter demands on their loyal civil servants had the intended effect.

THE ROAD TO DENMARK

Low corruption from the mid-1800s onwards meant much

more efficient tax collecting, as taxes began to provide a solid economic foundation for the embryonic Danish welfare state.

Efforts to minimise corruption roughly coincided with the early steps towards Danish representative government in the pre-constitutional period leading up to 1849. This concurrence of anti-corruption measures and a new breed of idealistic politicians entering the government structures probably helped keep corruption from becoming a serious problem in Denmark's political system, in contrast to a country like Italy. The difference today is striking. It would hardly surprise anyone – in Denmark or in Italy – to hear of an Italian politician who had links to organised crime or had accepted bribes from businessmen.

The vast majority of new politicians elected to sit in the first Danish parliamentary assembly of 1849 were former civil servants, today referred to as 'government officials'. They brought with them an anti-corruption culture, ingrained through their training and work. These very principles were further entrenched, decades later, in several ways. In 1919 came *Tjenestemandsloven* (the Public Servants Act), promoting the development of a well-run constitutional state, which also came to include a national audit authority, *Rigsrevisionen*, and the institution of the *Ombudsmand* (in the modern sense, the office of the 'public complaints investigator', whose title has ancient Norse roots). All of these things still benefit Denmark and its civil society today.

There is no doubt that solid, impartial, rule-based

institutions such as these, which rely on and enforce legislation, are the bodies we point to when social scientists, World Bank economists and others ask how Denmark became Denmark. But can, and should, this model be copied by other countries struggling against corruption?

I cannot recommend copying Denmark's road thus far, since that would mean installing a ruler with absolute power, engineering runaway inflation and undermining wages, not to mention provoking someone to bombard your capital city – twice, if you follow the model of Lord Nelson & Co. Calamities rarely reduce corruption in a country. Still, Denmark does prove it is possible to create a society with low corruption, despite a history of state bankruptcy and bloodshed. One crucial factor is probably a sustained will in the country's ruling body, be it autocratic or democratic, to quash corruption.

We must assume there are other options, aside from re-enacting the last few bloody, chaotic centuries of Danish history. At least so say the hopeful researchers, politicians and peoples who suffer daily under the destructive influences of corruption.

Arguably there is no quick fix or universal solution. We are nowhere near cracking the code, so for now, hold the champagne. Nevertheless, it seems that certain steps in Denmark's history, as outlined above, may point countries in the right direction.

Above all there must be a political will to clamp down on corruption, regardless of a wrongdoer's power or status. In Denmark the will was there, not just because Birch and others had broken the law while discharging their official duties, but because punishing corrupt actions was necessary for the kings to claim and uphold legitimacy. If ordinary citizens had not seen the law – Justitia, the Roman goddess of justice – as blind and therefore equally applicable to all, they might have turned their resentment and rage upon the king himself.

Once the political will is there, it is easier to recruit officials based on ability and not on connections, and then introduce a code of conduct supported by legal sanctions. Another factor is the importance of the population's ability to read and write. Citizens must be able to understand the laws of the land, but they must equally be able to notify the authorities of violations. They must also have recourse to some sort of complaints board or procedure that can test the authorities' actions and decisions. In a Danish context, the surge in literacy after the Lutheran Reformation in 1536 was a vital step. Martin Luther believed people ought to be able to read the Bible for themselves, and so the population had to learn to read.

In the early 1900s, Max Weber devised one of his 'ideal types' to describe a rational, effective bureaucracy – corruption-free, of course. Weber emphasised that the officials must be organised in a well-defined hierarchy with clear-cut tasks for each person; with objective qualification requirements; with a clear pay structure; and with a ban on mixing private and public funds. Interestingly, all of these measures had been introduced in Danish legislation, to a greater or lesser degree, before 1860.

PUBLIC ENEMY NO. 1

WITHOUT WILL, THERE IS NO WAY

Consider countries such as Venezuela, Libya and Turkmenistan, where corrupt regimes and public officials are the norm. What are they to do? They have just as many laws against corruption as Denmark does, but the realities of life there are completely different, and there are no easy solutions in sight. How can these countries defeat corruption if their rulers are at the root of it – holding the power to fight it, but behaving corruptly themselves? The answer is disheartening: There is little to be done.

In recent decades, several large international organisations have redoubled their efforts against corruption, trying to spur governments into action. In 2003 the UN adopted an anti-corruption convention meant to make such offences punishable by law, to ensure that perpetrators are actually prosecuted and to protect witnesses, experts and victims called upon to give evidence. Many countries have yet to sign the convention, so even the best-intentioned supranational efforts have little impact.

The World Bank and the IMF officially have a zero-tolerance policy on corruption, doing their best to strictly control accounting and enforce accountability in their partner countries. In 2013 the president of the World Bank even referred to corruption as "Public Enemy No. 1".

The EU has likewise thrown itself into the fray, setting up a large office in Brussels dedicated to investigating corruption. In 1999 the Council of Europe also set up the Group of States against Corruption (GRECO), an agency that supports anti-corruption work in the 49 member states. The effects of these initiatives are extremely hard to measure, but one thing is certain. Corruption is still alive and kicking in Europe, and the rest of the world.

Taking a long-term view, perhaps it would make a difference if we raised everyone's awareness of just how destructive corruption is? This might conceivably change the voting behaviour of ordinary citizens, which brings us to the next challenge. Ballot systems in many countries are rigged and electoral mechanisms flawed, not to mention that some dictatorships have no elections at all, so once again: What to do?

Scandinavians, from our lofty perch, might chirp: "Fight for democracy and human rights!" In the real world, however, democratic systems alone cannot lift countries out of corruption. They can boost positive trends, but the answer is much more complex.

SPRING WAS IN THE AIR

In December 2010 a dramatic suicide set a tidal wave of anti-corruption protests in motion. A desperate 26-year-old Tunisian named Mohammed Bouazizi set himself alight to demonstrate his utter exasperation with the pervasive abuses of power. Shortly before this act of self-immolation, the police, notoriously bent, had ruined Bouazizi's livelihood, confiscating all the fruit he was going to sell at the market. Lodging a complaint would have been useless and probably would have just made the young man's situation even worse.

During his 23 years in power Tunisia's president, Ben Ali, had installed a thoroughly corrupt regime. Dishonesty was endemic, and the president's extended family owned a good 20% of the companies in the country's private sector. They held monopolies on certain car brands and owned many of the country's radio and television stations, and legislation was systematically moulded in their favour.

Bouazizi's death triggered what came to be known as the Arab Spring. Thousands of Tunisians took to the streets, objecting against the regime's abusive practices. Their protests rippled across Egypt, Libya, Bahrain, Syria, Morocco, Saudi Arabia, Algeria and Kuwait. Here, too, the people demanded justice and equality under the law, regardless of connections and families ties.

The anger and frustration of ordinary people over their seemingly hopeless life situations, ineffective regimes, lack of democratic participation, poverty and high unemployment was profound and widespread. The contrast between their lives and those of the tiny, luxuriously cocooned upper class was shocking.

Imagine, for the sake of argument, that the billions of dollars siphoned off the world's official economies were somehow invested in clean drinking water, hospitals, education and infrastructure instead. What a change it would make in the daily lives of billions of people around the globe.

Researchers recently estimated that, worldwide, corruption has cost an astounding 3.6 million human lives. The dizzying sums drained from some the world's poorest countries could pay for 165 million vaccinations against measles, tetanus, tuberculosis and polio; medication for 11 million HIV / AIDS patients; and wages for half a million school teachers, who could educate ten million children.

Often, an official's or politician's own road to the profitable public office they hold – their meal ticket to the buffet of corruption – is paved with dubious methods and devious deals. Politicians buy votes for money or favours, or they offer administrative jobs to friends or sell them to the highest bidder. The road to power and influence is expensive, so once a person had achieved a lucrative position, they have to exploit it to recoup their losses. One 2016 estimate shows that in any given year, some 50 million people in the Middle East and North Africa will have paid a bribe.

The vicious circle becomes almost impossible to break, since no one has any personal financial interest in leading the fight. But the massive popular protests of the Arab Spring against dysfunctional and deeply corrupt national leadership did bring some hope, albeit small, of better times ahead.

New research from 2017 indicates just how difficult it is to break the insidious logic of corruption. Even so, the mere fact that the battle is endless is no reason not to fight – and revisiting the myth of Sisyphus, at least this unending struggle has a meaningful goal. The Middle East may still seem chaotic, but it is fair to hope that the Arab Spring was a wake-up call, at least for some of the powerful elite in that region, and in Asia as well. Although people are genuinely fed up, the question remains whether their anger and frustration can really put a lid on corruption.

TAKING TO THE STREETS

Skirmishes between police and demonstrators. Weeks-long blockades in city squares. A metropolis where protesters camp out for months on end. These may sound like Arab Spring scenes from Cairo or Tunis, but they occurred in New York City – in the very heart of America's financial district – late in the summer of 2011, when the Occupy Wall Street movement took to the streets.

The global financial crisis and its aftermath, in the US and elsewhere, brought to light a profusion of dirty deals and dubious practices in the private and public sectors. It also revealed blatant abuses of power and extreme greed in the world of finance and banking, with corporations and politicians conspiring to maximise personal gain at the expense of society as a whole.

Occupy Wall Street berated the establishment for the extreme social and economic inequality caused, in complicity, by America's politicians and businessmen during decades of exploitation and cover-ups. As a result, about 1% of the American population earns some 25% of total incomes and owns roughly 40% of the nation's total assets. This distribution of income and wealth is extremely skewed, especially seen from a Scandinavian perspective.

Sometimes the financial sector has verifiably spent huge sums to buy influence with politicians, either directly or through lobbyists or think tanks, making the subsequent political decision-making neither impartial nor transparent.

In 2001 the US company Halliburton, a large player in the oil and construction industries, was chosen to supply fuel to US forces in Iraq. No other companies were given a chance to bid for the contract. It later came to light that Halliburton had overcharged by more than 90% compared to market prices, evidently reasoning that with no competitors in sight the company might as well make the most of its favourable position.

By the same token, Halliburton won a contract to rebuild parts of Iraq's infrastructure – bridges, roads and oil refineries – to the tune of eight billion US dollars. The question is whether Halliburton would have been awarded the contract had it not donated millions of dollars to Republican presidential candidate George W. Bush's campaign in 2000. Incidentally, the director of Halliburton at the time was a man named Richard Cheney, a former US secretary of defence who later that year was chosen as Bush's running mate and ended up serving as vice-president for eight years. As far as watertight doors and arm's-length principles go, this does not paint a very trustworthy picture of the relations between corporate America and the nation's political system.

WARNING LIGHTS ON

SOMETHING ROTTEN INDEED

On 8 September 1908, a well-dressed gentleman stepped into the courthouse in Copenhagen. With a pair of pince-nez spectacles poised on his nose and a small, neatly trimmed moustache, P.A. Alberti, the Danish Minister of Justice, must have cut a fine figure as he told the duty officer he had come to turn himself in for corruption.

As chairman of the country's second-largest financial institution – the Zealand Farmers' Savings and Loan – Alberti had been running a bond scam for years. The proceeds, amounting to 16 million kroner and equalling 20% of Denmark's annual national revenue in 1908, had mainly been lost on ill-fated share investments in a South African gold mine.

In all fairness Alberti had used some of the money to fill a gaping hole in the accounts of the country's largest exporter of butter, a key Danish commodity. Very conveniently, Alberti was chairman of the company's board, and attempting to ensure voter support he had been paying Zealand dairy farmers more for their butter than the price it could fetch in England. In November 1910 the disgraced former minister of justice was sentenced to eight years in prison for his crimes.

Corruption is a sort of disease, a rot that is unavoidable in any type of political system or public administration, from ancient times up to the present. In modern Danish history, corruption did not end with the case against Minister Alberti. In the past few years the state of Denmark has seen the unravelling of several major scandals.

The most spectacular cases include the revelation a couple of years ago that Danske Bank, the largest bank in Denmark, had been involved in money laundering on an almost unfathomable scale. Between 2007 and 2015, an estimated 230 *billion* dollars' worth of funds had passed through the Danske Bank branch in Estonia, with transactions conducted for a number of clients from Russia and Azerbaijan, among other places. The funds, which had been earned illegally, needed credible provenance to look legitimate, and the Estonian branch of Danske Bank was happy to help provide this while receiving handsome fees for its services.

Another huge financial scam based in Denmark was discovered in 2015 when the State Prosecutor for Serious Economic and International Crime (the national fraud squad) began to investigate irregularities involving the Danish tax authorities. A tax employee had 'assisted' several ingenious (and presumably felonious) financiers by processing bogus documentation claiming refunds for share-dividend taxes paid to the Danish state. What has since become known as "the dividend scandal" involved payouts from Denmark of no less than 12 billion kroner (some 1.8 billion US dollars) to foreign companies.

Put simply, for several years these investors had been applying for tax refunds based on dividends from fictitious shareholdings. As a result, despite numerous warning lights flashing to alert the tax authorities that something was amiss, the companies had wrongly received enormous refunds. As of 2020, the labyrinthine clean-up operation is still ongoing.

On a smaller scale, a serious case of fraud was uncovered a few years ago at the National Board of Health and Welfare, where one entrusted employee had embezzled about 120 million kroner over a period of 25 years. Another large case at an IT company called ATEA, involving bribery and embezzlement from 2009 to 2014, incriminated several important employees. ATEA, which supplied IT infrastructure to the public sector, had provided public employees with gifts such as paid holidays and IT equipment. The Danish fraud squad ended up investigating nearly fifty government officials, who were later arrested and charged.

A MORAL COMPASS OUT OF KILTER?

Transparency International's 2019 corruption index ranked Denmark and New Zealand as the world's least corrupt nations, both scoring 87 out of 100 for shared first place – 100 being the ideal, corruption-free country. But in light of Denmark's even higher score of 92 back in 2014, it is evident that while our systems are working well, things are by no means perfect.

In other international ratings Denmark also scores

high on freedom of the press and on integrity in public administration. The 2017 World Governance Indicators, published by the World Bank, showed that for more than a decade Denmark had been at the high end in terms of controlling corruption and adhering to the rule of law. The general level of reported bribery is also low, according to surveys of Danish citizens and businesses, and the payment of bribes to access public benefits such as assistance from police, courts, and health and education services is extremely rare.

Even so, corrupt behaviour does occur, as it always has done, in Denmark and in every other country I can name. Corruption is everywhere. It is not something Denmark or other fortunate nations can relegate to the past; nor can it be stopped by borders. As evidenced by the examples above, it is very much a thing of the present.

Presumably, bent behaviour will always occur most among the rich and powerful. Sadly, today Lord Acton's observation that "power corrupts" remains as relevant as ever. In recent years, Danish members of parliament and ministers of state have also been entangled in a variety of gaffes and incidents that range from borderline amusing to awkward to downright suspicious – albeit not manifestly corrupt. So much for singing the praises of Denmark as a paragon of political propriety. New and different values seem to be spreading, slowly but surely, across this little land, seen by many as an exemplary nation built on trust, equality and ingrained integrity.

Nevertheless, Danish authorities and politicians

are not overly keen to strengthen the mechanisms that would increase compliance with GRECO's unambiguous messages, which notably recommend better whistle-blowing processes, more insight into politicians' financial interests and stricter codes of conduct for top executives.

One factor nudging the needle of Denmark's moral compass may be the way the country's public institutions are increasingly being run on market terms, with trends like New Public Management and performance metrics gaining ground. This blurs what was formerly a very clear distinction between public institutions and private organisations, a distinction traditionally upheld in Danish administration practices since the mid-1800s. This is a slippery slope. Suddenly, the top priority may not be the citizens' best interests, but one's own personal advantage, or a bigger salary. Another factor is that in this digital age, probing journalists and zealous citizens can more easily keep a watchful eye on the public sector, whereas they cannot demand the same level of transparency in the decision-making and business dealings of private companies.

In the current climate, confident, powerful politicians have a disproportionately large scope of action, which creates the potential for corruption. Although the problem in Denmark is much smaller than in most other countries, here, as elsewhere, there is good reason to remain vigilant and insist on government officials being professional, objective and profoundly respectful of the letter of the law

– qualities laboriously built up by absolutism over several centuries.

Let's face it: Humans are selfish. So to prevent people from unjustly enriching themselves, the playing field and the rules of the game must be firmly fixed and clearly communicated. An EU-funded research project finalised in 2017 showed that key elements in the battle against corruption include transparency, meritocratic recruitment, bureaucratic autonomy, high standards of accountability, strong political will and independent, impartial legal institutions. Indeed, as this Danish foray into corruption has shown, it takes a lot more than trust and good intentions to curb greed.